Y0-CAT-194

SHAPE UP OR SHIP OUT, BEETLE BAILEY

Here's the ninth in the happy series of books based on one of the most famous comic strips in the country. Once again the madcap gang from Camp Swampy strive valiantly to cope with their own ineptitude—and succeed in delighting us on every page.

Mort Walker again presents a hilarious collection of his marvelous cartoons depicting the most unprofessional soldier in the army!

Shape Up or Ship Out,

beetle bailey

by Mort Walker

tempo
books

GROSSET & DUNLAP, INC.

PUBLISHERS • NEW YORK

8-29

10-3

YOU **WILL** PUT LITTER IN THE **BASKET!!** BY ORDER OF GEN. HALFTRACK

I DUNNO.. IT SCARES ME!

Mort WALKER